GUIDED MEDI
SLEEP STORIES
FOR OLDER CHILDREN
and those young at heart
book 4

Welcome to these individual stories that are as individual as you!

Theodore Mann

author Linda Owen

LOwen

Published 2023 by Linda Owen the Author

An holistic approach to wellbeing

About this book!

Read each story together

Draw and colour me a picture to go with each individual story at the very end

Fall to sleep listening to each individual story again

Fill in the journal too about you!

THIS BOOK IS A TOOOL IN LIFE TOO

Also by Linda Owen

GUIDED MEDITATION SLEEP STORIES book 3

GUIDED MEDITATION SLEEP STORIES book 2

GUIDED MEDITATION SLEEP STORIES book 1

3 GIRLS 1 UNICORN

ME HABITS

THE HABIT FAMILY

THE HABIT

POETRY DRIFTNG THROUGH LIFE

WISDOM

GUIDED MEDITATIONS SPIRITUAL AND PRACTICAL

OUR BILLY

THE BLACK SHEEP OF THE FAMILY

LIVING IN POETRY

DEDICATION

To all the children who love stories and those encouraged or introduced to them. Amongst my meditation work for adults it is an extra delight to address children's needs when it's time to enter sleep - that passage through the night. I hope these stories are of great comfort and inspire your positive imagination that's simply magical!

Did you know kids whose mothers and fathers read to them are proven to handle entering school life better with less aggression or inattention such as ADHD. You are also creating a safe place to feel loved and valued in a world that is ever changing.

If you read slowly pausing with this script allowing a positive imagination with their breathing too will help them settle and we are creating a good bedtime routine to sustain a healthy mind and body.

These stories are also in audio style on Insight Timer with me plus I have many more for adults too.

Thank you xx

GUIDED MEDITATION SLEEP STORIES FOR CHILDREN

Are you ready to be read to by a parent or a trusted friend? Here is teamwork for each story is read at a steady pace whilst you the little listener close your eyes and imagine it all. By the time the story is complete it will lead you into pleasant dreams and going to bed will be magic!

Don't forget the other activities in this book too xx

Hey I would love your feedback by leaving a book review with thanks from me to you x

CONTENT

DREAMS CAN BE FUN

Welcome to this guided sleep meditation
Called **Dreams Can Be Fun**
Let's begin
So before you get into bed
Make that pillow super fresh and squeeze it tight
Refresh the pillow then jump into bed
Settle into bed now
Closing one eye to sleep
Closing the next eye to dream big
Let the eyes inside go round and round, round
Please tense the feet for a few seconds
Tensing next the long legs
Tense now a few seconds the abdomen
Now tense arms hands shoulders
Lastly tense the face a few seconds
Give your whole body permission to rest and recharge
Relax those eyes
Please empty your mind 10 seconds now thank you
....
Let's make this bedroom dreamy
Imagine
Every bedroom wall the floor the ceiling turning star bright
Like the room is a big star in the sky
It is a very sleepy star bright bedroom
That takes you up into the night sky
Floating this entire bedroom up to join the stars in the sky
We need to start this journey from a moment of peace silence and stillness

We need to breathe into star light
Be surrounded by the highest of dreamy fluffy clouds
That cushion all of you
The lightness of air of the natural wind
The lightness of thick huge white clouds
And the lightness of a galaxy of stars
May a super moon shine onto all your bedroom in this sky
Breathe into dreams
And ready for a fun adventure to take you further now
A moon star bright dragon, is coming very soon to bond with you
A night friend that is great at wishing for wonderful things for your future
So get ready by creating an energy smile that starts
From a gentle smile on your face
Eyes that smile
A heart that smiles by simply opening up
The body the aura vibrates an energy smile
The night star dragon is ready for you now
You may pick a name for him be creative have fun
Let a name pop in your head now
....
Feel your heart is listening to the heart of this dragon
And then you are lifted onto his back as you begin very much a fun adventure

A bright dragon star bright flies you both incredibly fast straight out into the universe
He's going to teach you about the magic of thoughts and creation
Of which this energy itself is super bright full of life
He makes you look down also at earth and wants you to see that earth
Is the only planet that supports life physical life that is
But up here are the ingredients to make new things
The biggest things to happen start here in the universe
Many tiny planets fill the great universe, and both shall do some planet hopping tonight!
There is time to go now to the planet of islands
Hundreds of islands for a much needed tonic for you both
The weather the colours are individual to each island
Your first stop is a stormy island
Just because it's exciting to feel the elements making you feel fresh and alive
Time to watch big waves super-fast winds
And get the biggest energy cleanse you can imagine
Sounds fill the head the ears like a big orchestra
The sky colours are ever changing
So embrace it all
And when you've been here for a while

Ask your dragon to find something totally, different again
Such as a crystal planet
Like sparkling diamonds with an extra kick of energy super powers
Healing and empowering you
Take your time of course
Enjoy and enjoy it all
Now

DRAW WHAT YOU SAW
IN **DREAMS CAN BE FUN**

POWER COLOUR DRAGON

Welcome to this guided sleep meditation
Called **Power Colour Dragon**
Let's begin
So before you get into bed
Make that pillow super fresh and squeeze it tight
Refresh the pillow then jump into bed
Settle into bed now
Closing one eye to dream
Closing the next eye for the Power Colour Dragon
Let the eyes inside go up and down up down
Please tense the feet a few seconds
Now tense next the long legs
Tense now a few seconds the abdomen
Now tense arms hands shoulders
Relax the eyes now
As you tense the face for 10 seconds now
....
Give your whole body permission to rest and recharge
Please empty your mind 10 seconds now thank you
....
Let's make this bedroom dreamy
Imagine
Every bedroom wall the floor the ceiling turning as bright as a star
Like the room is a big star in the sky
It is a very dreamy star bright bedroom
That lifts you up into the night sky
Floating this entire bedroom up to join the stars in the sky

We need to start this journey from a moment of peace
We need to breathe into star light
Be surrounded by the highest of dreamy fluffy clouds
That cushion all of you
The lightness of air of the natural wind
The lightness of huge white brilliant white clouds
And the lightness of a galaxy of stars
May a super moon shine onto all your bedroom in this sky
Breathe into super white moon light
And ready for a fun adventure to take you further now
A Power Colour Dragon is coming very soon to bond with you
A night friend that is a good friend creating a wonderful future for you
So get ready by creating an energy smile that starts
From a gentle smile on your face
Eyes that sparkle with a smile
A heart that smiles by simply opening up
The body the aura vibrates an energy smile
The Power Colour Dragon is ready for you now
You may pick a name for him be creative have fun
Let a name pop in your head now
. . .
Feel your heart is listening to the heart of this colourful dragon
And then you are lifted onto his flying back

There are hundreds of colours on this dragon
as you begin very much a big colourful adventure
And flies you both incredibly fast straight out into the universe
He's going to teach you about the magic of thoughts and creation
Of which this energy itself is super bright full of life
He makes you look down also at earth and wants you to see that earth
Is the only planet that supports physical life that is
But up here are the ingredients to make new things
The biggest things to happen start here in the universe
He smiles back on earth
Because the connection of colour
There was a time when all televisions were still only in black and white for example
Meaning earth continues evolving
Now many different planets fill the universe
Time to visit time for planet hopping fun
The 1st planet to stop is all about colours
This is why the Power Colour Dragon is here for you
This is exciting it's bit like going to a party
For when we celebrate things we lean on colour it's inspiration
When you land here you feel an amazing reaction on every level
The planet oozes colour and you are made aware you too have a strong

Connection to colour
To feel everything about you starts spinning is really uplifting
Thus lifting your vibration
Colours work on many levels
The physical the emotional the mental
Colours nourish you and complete you
Anything on an old slow vibration
Just can't stay anymore with you
You start the colour planet adventure treatment
For you shall breath colour
Smell it eat it drink it and play upon it
Slide down colourful slides and tunnels
Bounce on it
Swim in colour
Fly in it
Send the body into happiness
Copy your Power Colour Dragon if you please
Breathe in orange
Take a lick on the lips of red
Eat some purple
Slide down the green slide
Flying in blues and pinks
It's very much a party planet but is so good for you
Plus everything looks so pretty in a good way
May all this beauty reflect inside of you
For that feels powerful
Here upon this colour planet all your energies reveal their colours
They are simply going to get brighter and stronger
And doing it with fun

Open your eyes wide to every colour that presents itself to you
By the time you leave this planet you shall
Have a hundred colours upon you
Like the Power Colour Dragon
And then only then will you hop to somewhere different to follow
For planet hopping is sheer fun
So with all my heart to yours get busy with colour fun
Together you look amazing
Bond well with your great friend
Dream big

DRAW WHAT YOU SAW
IN **COLOUR POWER DRAGON**

THE ISLAND CHAMPION

Welcome to this guided sleep meditation
Called **The Island Champion**
Let's begin
Please prepare your pillow and squeeze it tight make it nice and dreamy
Into bed now
Get comfortable
Closing one eye for the Island Champion
Closing the next eye for your own dream boat to get there
Let the eyes inside go round and round like an island sitting surrounded by water
Islands are wonderful so much to experience here
Let the eyes rest and relax
Connect to your bed how it supports all your body
Just like a little boat would do upon a sea
May your bed turn into a boat
At the count of 3
123
Such a beautiful magical boat
So clean so loved by you
It glows so bright attached to it is 2 fireflies that go everywhere with it
Is your bed swaying to the rhythm of the sea
Does the sea air make you feel a live and strong at heart?
Yes even your breathing is like the sea of in and out moving and flowing
Your boat has feelings and is most excited to take you to the island champion
But before you get there

What sea animals or birds would you like to spot
before you get there
Please have half a minute now and feast your eyes
on a wonderful sea friend if you please
. . .
As with all these island stories it is nightfall
The boat is in a way lit up by stars that mirror
themselves on the ocean surface
If there is a moon this time it will become 2 moons
One in the sky as you look up
One below sea level as you look down
This lovely moon stays with you like a torch as you
travel smoothly to this island
The 2 fireflies love to glow when it's a little dark so
with the magic of nature they shine bright green
It a long journey but it's great to have a snack and
drink upon your boat
Time to enjoy something savoury and then
something sweet
Have half a minute relaxing and enjoying life
Can you hear your boat making a squeaky noise
The boat announces you are here now
It's time to put your invisible cloak on just for a
while whilst you investigate this island
Your magic cloak also tells the boat to be invisible
too
And to wait for your safe and happy return
So what is this island all about ?
Best jump onto the sandy beach and watch the sky
announce a new morning

It's very early and the sun is beginning yes beginning to rise slow and steady
Please stand on the sand as you get your land legs back after all that sea travel
Have half a minute here and what do you like and makes you smile?
Remember you are invisible so time to look around which means also to look
Also to listen
Also to smell whatever catches your nose
Also to listen to your inner gut feelings
Here comes the island people they are singing as they walk
The females have flowers in their hair
The males have feathers in their hair
Someone blows a horn
And many swim so fast it looks like a race
Notice some are faster than others
But the race is long it seems
Now others are catching up then someone takes the lead
As the race comes to an end one winner steps out the water
Time to take a closer look
How did he win what does it take to win a long race?
But because you have an invisible cloak on it can also look deep into another's life
So you sit back and watch the life story of the winner at swimming

It turns out that from a young age it was his favourite exercise
He had no interest in running or weight lifting or karate
So from a young age he first swam for fun and to let off some steam
Whenever he felt worried or stressed by challenges in life
He felt swimming made him feel clean and like a fresh start
The water the sea itself he thought was the most beautiful thing he had seen
Even relaxing and just observing the way it moved
He was also very creative and tried many different ways to move in the water
Having a good healthy body meant he drank plenty of water
And eats regular with a balanced diet
He also slept well which helps everything in the day time being alert
Most of all a passion and enjoyment to this type of sport
He loves it completely and so this made him a winner
The others didn't quite have this
Some said I don't love this sport
Or I don't have time to practice
My taste for certain foods aren't healthy and so on
I hope you will remember the secret of this island
Champion
That makes him a winner at swimming

Would you like to reveal yourself and join in a celebration?
Which will be a big party of the winner
On the beach
It would be nice to make some island friends and explore the island as a guest too
And so you take your invisible cloak off
Smile and be greeted as a guest
As a guest you are decorated with a choice of flowers or feathers
Shake the hand of the champion called Bookar
Suddenly the beach is busy as everyone helps out
A fire to be made and to dance and sit around for later
Fresh foods for the biggest picnic on the beach
Lovely fruity exotic drinks
Flowers everywhere
There shall be singing and musical instruments like drums and flutes
So enjoy this then after go back to your very own boat and return after the party
Home sweet home for the next adventure to come
Enjoy this island dream

DRAW WHAT YOU SAW
IN **THE ISLAND CHAMPION**

THE ISLAND OF WISDOM

Welcome to this guided sleep meditation
Called **The island of Wisdom**
Let's begin
Please prepare your pillow and squeeze it tight make it nice and dreamy
Into bed now
Get comfortable
Closing one eye for the island of wisdom
Closing the next eye for your own dream boat to get there
Let the eyes inside go round n round like an island sitting surrounded by water
Islands are wonderful so much to experience here
Let the eyes rest and relax
Connect to your bed how it supports all your body
Just like a little boat would do upon a sea
May your bed turn into a boat
At the count of 3
123
Such a beautiful magical boat
So clean so loved by you
It glows so bright attached to it is 2 fireflies that go everywhere with it
Is your bed swaying to the rhythm of the sea
Does the sea air make you feel alive and strong at heart
Yes even your breathing is like the sea the rhythm of in and out moving and flowing
Your boat has feelings and is most excited to take you to the island of wisdom

But before you get there what sea animal or bird
would you like to spot before you get there
Please have half a minute now and feast your eyes
on a wonderful sea friend if you please
....
As with all these island stories it is nightfall
The boat is in a way lit up by stars that mirror
themselves on the ocean surface
If there is a moon this time it will become 2 moons
One in the sky as you look up
One below sea level as you look down
This lovely moon stays with you like a torch as you
travel smoothly to this island
The 2 fireflies love to glow when it's a little dark so
with the magic of nature they shine bright green
It a long journey but it's great to have a snack and
drink upon your boat
Time to enjoy something savoury and then
something sweet
Have half a minute relaxing and enjoying life
Can you hear your boat making a squeaky noise
The boat announces you are here now
It's time to put your invisible cloak on just for a
while whilst you investigate this island
Your magic cloak also tells the boat to be invisible
too
and to wait for your safe and happy return
So what is this island all about ?
Best jump onto the sandy beach
and watch the sky announce a new morning

It's very early and the sun is beginning yes
beginning to rise slow and steady
Please stand in the sand as you get your land legs
back after all that sea travel
Have half a minute here and what do you like and
makes you smile
Remember you are invisible so time to look around
which means also to look
Also to listen
Also to smell whatever catches your nose
Also to listen to your inner gut feelings
Here comes the island people
They are celebrating something and time to take a
closer look
Well the entire population have come down to the
beach
And begin to make the biggest circle of life
Each must take their turn to walk to the centre and
do something
So in fact because you are invisible you may go to
the centre
and get the up close look at the fine details
So someone carries a lighted torch to celebrate
fire
A ripple of hand waves goes round this circle as if
all were suddenly just one big giant thing
It's looks like a magic spectacular fun game
But really although they are island people they
simply understand the gift of life
Oneness how each other is connected and affected
by each other

Through the journey of life
As the person with the fire leaves the centre of the circle
Then another rushes in with a large dish of water
And again a ripple of hand waves goes round this circle
So they must be celebrating and connecting to gratitude
Remember what we focus on in a way increases becomes stronger and yes abundant too
The island people are using the basics of magic
They are treasuring everything that is good
So the next person to rush to the centre of the circle
She is carrying soil with a small plant growing on top of it
The circle of people do another magic hand wave
This celebration continues and continues
There is also some unique moments
For some of them have found new things on the island
For climbing and foraging is encouraged if you are fit of course
Seeing something new together is of great interest
it reminds them how creative and alive earth really is
Now the oldest person walks to the centre
For this too is to be celebrated
The old lady tells everyone to sit down and listen
She wishes to bring one topic of old age to enlighten the others

She tells of no matter what worrying is a waste of time
Many times in life worry looked her in the eye and she simply said
No
She only put her good energies on going forwards
Using logic and a good sense of humour
Now is it time to reveal yourself and take your invisible cloak off
And be welcomed by the islanders
For they wish to explain their celebration is done every month
They will never take anything for granted but choose to grateful for all they have
Which seems to keep it all growing very well
It is an abundant island
A lucky necklace is decided to be given as a gift to you
It is very natural made of shells and string grass
When they put you in the circle and it is placed upon you
They do once more the hand wave all around you
The energy of this unity almost makes the necklace jingle from sheer vibrations
Of happiness of Gratitude and focused energy
So as you go back to your boat
They bring food and drink to take for the journey home
And push your boat out into the blue sea
Singing a goodbye song that carries on the wind

You can't stop feeling so happy for in this moment all is so wonderful
The sun does shine
The sea is gentle
You are nourished feeling lucky
And have learnt how to be grateful for all amazing things
Well relax in to the great dreamland
For a new day and new things to discover and treasure

DRAW WHAT YOU SAW
IN **ISLAND OF WISDOM**

THE FANCY DRESS STORY

Welcome to this guided sleep meditation
Called **The Fancy Dress Story**
Let's begin
Please prepare your pillow and squeeze it tight
Make a dreamy fluffy tonight
Settle into bed now
Closing one eye to sleep
Closing the next for fancy dress fun
Let the eyes inside
Look left as if staring at outfits you'd like to try on
Let the inside go right as if staring at another outfit you'd love to try on
Settle the eyes let the fun begin
Now tense all the face tight thinking how many outfits can I dream in this dream of fun
Relax all of you
Wishing but also asking for a personal assistant with many outfits
Your own PA to bring many wonderful great clothes from many great people
Your personal assistant must be very clever very loyal and sort out all the costumes as such
So the first big, huge box like a present is laid at your feet
As you dismiss your PA and take your first peek
Removing the lid box
And at first all you can see is gold and huge diamonds
Therefore this outfit belongs to either a queen or king

It a heavy crown but you will manage for it feels very special
There is a robe too super long and very warm
With black and white marking
Now is it a dress or a suit you find next?
Quick decide are you a king or a queen
Don't forget the shoes
Time to put all of this together on you
You have half a minute thank you
Please go sit at your important desk
There are papers to sign and appointments that require your prescience
You will have to decide as you ring the bell if you are to travel by coach or a private plane
As you leave the room every door is opened with a smile and a bow
I want you to do something royal today
You have a minute to make something big happen now
. . .
Now your PA is ready to present a new box of clothes
So back in that bed and ring that bell
For a new box is to be put at your feet
Dismiss your PA with thanks and open the lid of the box
There's a black but shiny silver hat a helmet
It is a Policeman's helmet
Inside the hat is a name tag of a horse
A police horse that must be yours
There is a deep blue outfit

And a s special belt with many pockets
Things like handcuff, radio, flash light, baton, gloves, pencil, keys, multi-tools and so on
Dismiss your PA and put everything on
And now go find that police horse you are on duty keeping the peace
Have a minute now and think like a police person
Now it is back to the bedroom
Ring the bell then in comes your PA carrying a new box
Laid at your feet and Dismiss politely
As you lift the lid and find on top some keys for driving a fast car
There are lots of leather really padded heavy clothes to protect you
And sun glasses to protect your eyes
Well it looks like you are going to enter a big race
And your fast car awaits you
I wonder what colour it is and just how fast will you go to win the race of course?
There will a huge silver trophy as well plus a big cash prize
Go have some fun and I shall leave you for a minute good luck
And now for last one from me
So ring that bell and in comes your PA carrying a heavy box
Dismiss kindly and take the lid off the box off
Well the clothes look very old fashioned indeed
They kind of go back in time
There is an eye patch

A coloured head scarf
A gold earring
Shirt and trousers
Some big boots too
This must be an old pirate so there must be a ship waiting outside
Quick get dressed and go look at the window for the biggest and most fantastic ship ever
Lots of people wave at you, it must be your crew
So off you go and set sail very very soon
Into the cabin and look at your map as usual
Decide decide where this big ship huge ship is going and for what
But wait I shall let you complete this story journey as a pirate yourself
But remember
Dream big

DRAW WHAT YOU SAW
IN **FANCY DRESS STORY**

CLOUD STORY

Welcome to this guided sleep meditation
Called **Cloud Story**
Let's begin
Pillows love to be dreamy
So squeeze your pillow tight make a dream pillow
Settle into bed now
Get comfortable relax all the body
Go soft like a fluffy pillow and like a fluffy cloud
Close one eye for the sky
Close the next eye for100s of clouds
Remember each day we may do many things the same
But the clouds in sky will always look different each day
So I hope after this story you will enjoy noticing great exciting cloudy skies
Let the eyes inside go up
For wherever we go let the big sky always say hello
Look at me for I am ever ever changing
Relax your eyes time to dream
Maybe you will one day or have indeed
Also look down onto the magic clouds
Flying is something we like to do such as a big holiday
And with this windows round or long and thin are on the flying plane
To be in the sky is big magic
Excites the eyes as you can imagine only this time you look down at the clouds
Clouds do reach amazing heights to be so close very close

Grownups always look to the sky and talk about the weather
Every day the weather man talks about the sky
But when we are young we can get lost in the dreamworld of clouds
Have you ever seen huge, gigantic white clouds float and fly in the blue sky?
As you begin to stare all kinds of shapes are made from clouds
Giants with huge faces or angels on wings look into your very soul
Then there are baby clouds
That look like they are trying to catch up all the big important clouds
On a very windy day the clouds race and race across the sky
The windy breeze reaches us all on the ground
Faces react when the big grey clouds even black
For they are full of rain and thunder
I love myself to sit in a window in the home with my hot cocoa
And watch a big rain pour that often starts with thunder
The sky becomes a show sound fills the air
Waiting for the first rain to fall and wind throws it left and right onto my window
Storms take time and I am dry but watch it all from the window
Dark blueness and the sky becomes completely one big cloud
All that water must be released

The raindrops are fast and look so pretty they jump and bounce on the floor
On every surface it touches
The rain patterns are strong too tiny water circles from every rain drop as you stare and stare
Although very wet is so pretty
Lots of puddles will remain after the rain
Perfect for a good rain splash walk later
Have you ever had a picnic where you lie completely down?
And give the sky all your attention
Then the fun begins for clouds begin to speak to your imagination
Some clouds are so very white so clean and make those pictures in the sky
Faces like gods even big animals appear
Then next to them grey and blue clouds move around them
The movement can be so gentle and slow
As your eyes follow and follow until out of sight
Dragon clouds can be spotted for they are so long and pretty with a big head and a long tail
But what does it feel like to be on a cloud?
They look comfortable too like the inside of your pillow
If only you could ride one and because they are so high in the sky
They really can go round and round the world
Let's become a cloud friend
Think and feel as light as air
Think and feel super soft

Your whole body turning into a cloud itself
Such softness and so slow you move as you rise and rise heading to the sky
Straight as an arrow you go straight up into the biggest of skies
Until you reach all the other clouds
Now for the fun
Feast your eyes on a beautiful cloud and claim it
Smile and befriend the wind
Let the huge cloud and wind start a wonderful sky ride
And have a great journey flying round the world round the earth
You can easily and smoothly float over all the countries below you
Earth looks so small when you are cloud flying
Mountain, fields, lakes and rivers look so different from up here
The people look like tiny dots colourful toy people walking about
Ships look so small looking too
But everything is busy and colourful
The sky of clouds can feel very peaceful floating on the currents of the wind
It's bit like being on holiday a cloud holiday
So enjoy sightseeing for up here you can see everything
Clouds are beautiful and you are a cloud yourself
Take your time and drift and ride the sky
And when you feel so relaxed then you can sleep

On the best bed ever a cloud bed fluffy all the way
up to your chin
Now you might as well add some stars to sleep
your very best
Millions of stars are up here
And star light sparkles from each star
Moon bright lights up the clouds too into slivery
clouds and go very well together
They look and feel most wonderful
May you dream the lightest most magical sleep,
goodnight little cloud

DRAW WHAT YOU SAW
IN **CLOUD STORY**

THE COLOURFUL AUTUMN CHAKRA TREE

Welcome to this guided sleep meditation
Called **The Colourful Autumn Chakra Tree**
Let's begin
Please prepare your pillow squeezing it tightly let's create a super soft pillow
. . .
Let the body before you sleep
Have a good squeeze of all your body muscles
Like the changing autumn trees let the body change for a moment
Into a tight ball of all those muscles
Are you ready to fully relax laying down into bed ?
Rest deep into the pillow
Closing the eyes thank you
Allow the eyes inside begin to free flow left right up and down round and round
As you continue to get ready for some autumn colour energy
Take a full breath in and fully exhale
Let the eyes settle
As if looking straight ahead at a special autumn chakra tree
Let this big tree talk to your heart about autumn magic
This tree will not stay green for it is changing in a beautiful way
Have you noticed on autumn days how the sun lights everything up stronger?
Let the sunshine enter this big green tree completely

Watch and just know all the green leaves hundreds begin to change
Like hundreds of green lights
A very bright lit up green tree
Imagine breathing into this green bright energy colour straight into the heart area
For the heart radiates the colour green known as chakras
Boosting the centre of your heart with the power and flow of love
But the air is cool and as you breath in and out the air turns to white fog
Body fills up too with white, white fog
Breath in and out whiteness
Autumn brings a freshness that is simply uplifting refreshing
Stay with this big green tree as it begins its autumn colours
All the green leaves turning completely yellow
Breathe in yellow
See the sunshine lights up hundreds of yellow leaves like yellow lights
And your tummy is soothed and nourished by yellow
For the tummy radiates and connects to yellow energy
A big autumn strong wind cold super fresh fills you up with clean energy
And all the yellow leaves begin to float and float to the ground
And captures all of you

Filling your aura with golden yellow energy
Shining a big ball of golden yellow
Then they begin to change to another colour that is orange
Breathe through the nose and watch orange colour energy
Orange air connects to your hip area
Your orange chakra soothing, nourishing and comforting
Sunshine burns the orange into bright solid red leaves
And your feet begin to absorb the red energy colour that travels up the legs
Filling up with red, red energy
Unblocking any fear with stable and centred
Eventually all leaves go golden brown and shine and shine golden brown
As you connect to a grounding feeling of your roots
Your roots
That balance and support all of you
You decide to deepen your roots snugly into earth
And the deeper you go the more supported the more taller one feels
Posture and balance increases
Now your head feels it's touching the sky full of blue colours
And purple rays of light
Connecting beautifully to your higher chakras
Breathing in sky blue and breathe purple rays
Stepping into your power your creativity

Rise into a smile and feel it will reenergise you for you are energy
Sealing in now these extraordinary, beautiful autumn colours into your energy field
Feeling nourished so bright full of autumn colours
Take a full breath in and full breath out with thanks to this big autumn tree
Enjoy the rest of this sleep meditation of all the autumn memories you have deeply loved
Keep dreaming and treasure autumn
You decide if you are with someone or just nature
Dream of a big beautiful fresh autumn adventure
Dream big

DRAW WHAT YOU SAW
IN **THE COLOURFUL AUTUMN CHAKRA TREE**

I CONNECT TO THE BUTTERFLY

Welcome to this guided sleep meditation
Called **I connect to the butterfly**
Let's begin in your bedroom
Please squeeze your pillow make a dreamy pillow
. . .
Please get comfortable into bed now
Blink your eyes like the softness of butterfly wings
Then close and shut your eyes for dreaming
And I invite you to picture the image of any butterfly you wish
As you hold that breath still for 5 seconds now
Feel the breath slowly breath out
Let's deepen the connection to the butterfly
And understanding the image connected with each 4 stages of its life
Before it takes flight in the big world
Yes the 4 stages the egg the caterpillar the chrysalis & finally the butterfly
So butterlies are not only pretty to look at but also have meaning
Transformation, hope and change
The magnificent yet short life of the
very butterfly serves to remind us that life is short
Even minor changes can trigger what is also referred to as the butterfly effect
Breathe into the butterfly effect
In that small wing span of flutters can have indeed an impact on the world's weather
Example a butterfly flapping its wings in
South America
Can affect the weather in Central Park.

And what would happen if there were no butterflies?
Without them, there would simply be
no chocolates to enjoy no apples to crunch
And other foods that have become our daily comforts
Almost 75 % of the food crops worldwide depend on these pollinators
Now please picture the Monarch butterfly of orange and black lacey wings
For example travels great distances every year
It does so for warmer weather
Each year in October, Monarch butterflies migrate South and West for warmer weather
The discovery that this tiny butterfly can migrate nearly 2,500 miles from Europe
Flying high over the Mediterranean Sea, North Africa's mountains and the Sahara Desert
Yes this humble butterfly reaches heights of a mere mile or 2 in the air
Catching that air currant that the world is made of
So let's begin with the butterfly in you
And how significant is the first cycle the egg
How this relates to being born and being born to parents to the family tree your roots
And as we absorb like a sponge a lot of belief systems of how things are or should be
What is wonderful though the journey of life is indeed about change
And changes through time itself remember life is all about change

So the egg of the butterfly moves onto the 2nd cycle the caterpillar
And here we are moving through life and hungry for it
We are full of adventure as young ones and some lessons of life
Some paths in life are not all roses
So we are in as sense finding out about life and finding out about ourselves
And I love the very word gifts finding out what your gifted at
And then we do in a way work and serve each other
At what we are good or passionate about
There is no age limit too as to when one will shine
And know this is the real happy self, doing what brings joy pride and rewards
For the next cycle the caterpillar enters the third stage the cocoon
After all that moving around and feasting on food and life itself
A time to go within and decide what you really will finally finally become
For when this cycle is completed you really can fly like the butterfly
And such a strong statement gaining your wings
Wings that are often decorated in many colours tells the world who you are now
And so another journey that seems no bounds
For you are not crawling around as such

You are lifted to a higher vibration and really can fly
For some it's this time when many things have already happened
And you know yourself better & even the downs have given you skills to be stronger
Gaining your tools so to speak
Let's connect to the breath once more by holding it still for 5 seconds now
Feel that breath smooth and long
Picturing now your own butterfly journey
The images in the mind of d great butterfly
That is yourself with these 4 stages in life
So connect first now to that egg
Picture your egg It's ok not to see perfection acknowledge any flaws in that egg
But you are ever changing into greatness
So please change that image to a sound happy egg right now
Connect to the 2nd stage the caterpillar
Picture your caterpillar again it's ok not to see perfection
And acknowledge here any flaws at this stage of life
But you are ever changing into greatness
So please change that image to a sound happy caterpillar now
Connect thirdly to that cocoon yours
Look acknowledge for it's still ok not to see perfection
But you are ever changing into greatness

So please change that image to a sound happy cocoon now
Finally the 4th stage connect to that butterfly
your wings appearing and unfolding
Out of the cocoon again it's ok not to see perfection
Then ready because I'm telling you are great at changing
So change that image to a happy sound butterfly now
Now see your butterfly wings opening again
Breathe deeply into these precious wings
Breathe into your unique colours again and your unique patterns
Be aware how powerful you are with flight as your direction
Watch your butterfly wings simply come alive
Thinking of all the things you love from the heart to be
Let the butterfly fly around you in sheer happiness
Now ask this wonderful butterfly to land on your human head
And feel it softly there
Let it feed the mind magical ways of how to live and reach those heights in life
Feel playful capture the image of your
unique butterfly into your higher heart
Let it remind you how beautifully gifted and unique you are
And each of us are

Feel a powerful peace in your being that sings the song of life
That we are equal in that we all are great at something
We all serve each other with our own unique gifts
And for a moment see millions upon billions of butterflies becoming one
And how successful they are at moving up and forwards in this world in this life
This makes the world a beautiful powerful wonderful place to live each day in
Now your wings may be delicate because they belong to a higher vibration of lightness
To reach such amazing heights in this world
And you have the tools to be a great butterfly
Let's seal this in physically now
Just allow the physical fingers to move and flutter freely
And with a physical slow stretch and with the human arms in slow motion style
Rise your arms like 2 wing sealing in and connected to butterfly
Let's awaken to the count of 7
1234567
Waking up now unfolding the body
Opening your beautiful eyes
Eyes wide open full of life
Thank you

DRAW WHAT YOU SAW
IN **I CONNECT TO THE BUTTERFLY**

I CONNECT TO MY INNER JOY AND STRENGTH

Welcome to this guided meditation
Called **I connect to my inner joy and strength**
Let's begin
Seated or lay down if you wish
Closing one eye thank you
Closing the next eye too
Holding the breath for 5 seconds now
Feel that breath and connect to smooth long breaths
Let the physical body get comfortable and still now
So the aim of this guided meditation is to awaken the extraordinary creativity The playful and most uplifting qualities of you
To balance out all the other stuff we call work chores responsibilities
And how this lightens the load of life itself keeping a healthy strong balance
As a child you have a set of tools and a deep connection
To seeing the world more with wonder the act of believing in the magical side Of things that lifts one to a higher place
For the heart can really hit the high notes of joy
And often turning things into a game and no longer a chore
So the art of relying on ourselves and ignite those precious qualities
Think how often you did laugh the innocence of looking for goodness
The vibration of love

So welcome to a special journey of connecting and making a fantastic bond With you
Let's expand that meditated mind
And imagine day dreaming and here you are but now we call it meditation
So please picture now your inner child of joy and strength
Is in a sense waiting for a private meeting almost sacred
At the top of a sacred mountain for you
Mountains in a way are symbolic of going deep into yourself for answers
A place far away
And also the curious inner child
With all those whys and how questions
Where do mountains come from in the first place?
The earth's crust is made of 6 gigantic plates
That fit together like a jigsaw
When 2 gigantic plates move through time
They can collide into each other
That pushes the earth's crust up forming mountains
I like how the word jigsaw is mentioned
Life does seem like a jigsaw puzzle
Getting all the jigsaw pieces to fit
Putting life into a big picture
And dramatic changes can bring positives too
For that new mountain born may give
Home to new plants
A place of security for animals
And a climb for the real mountaineers

So I invite you to awaken your inner joy and strength
Simply connecting straight away
Of you being bare feet how much your feet have yet to grow
For when the walk up this mountain begins soon
It is to be felt every step with your bare feet
And for now see yourself at the beginning stood under a big old apple tree
Breath in the smell of ripe fruits lingering in the air golden yellow ripe apples
See the tree as a gift
See the solid strength of its trunk
See the flexible branches
Feel the roots you just know are in the ground
And the crown that is bathed in sunshine.
Pick this live fruit of 2 shiny yellow apples as a gift to share later
And put them in your pocket for now
Be aware how flat the ground is when you compare this to the mountain
That is yet to be climbed
And although there is great comfort of the flat ground here
There is more on offer of which is reconnecting
To the extraordinary uplifting qualities of your own inner joy and strength
Be aware how mighty and tall this mountain is presented to you
Reflect on this mountain
Like the mountains in life

Sometimes mountains require a lot of energy
Mountains are about overcoming obstacles
To overcome the illusions of fear and stagnation
Of doubts and overthinking
But the rewards of the mountain climbed are magnificent......
Finding your joy and strength seeing the real you
So ready to go and meet your best friend that is you
Take that last look around as you leave this old apple tree
And taking that first step up the mountain...
Allow the feet the skin to hug to each climb
Get to know this mountain
Feel the hands are working with you
And all the body is gently flowing gracefully up this mountain
Start to feel the breath is working with you
Each step forward each breath
Each step up each breath
Have a moment connecting to this mountain that wants to be climbed...
Listen to that inner joy and strength whispering in your ear
Wishing for the wind to guide you to the top
Just because we can still wish.
So forwards with the help of a wind flowing in your direction
Feeling that current of air helping just a little.
And connecting to the strength of this mountain
In your hands and on the souls of the feet

Feel that body and even the toes pushing
With a rhythm of pushing you up and up
Remember all work is rewarded life is work and life has rewards
Your inner child may whisper again in your ear
To begin to hmm or sing to yourself as you use to do
When your heart is happy
And make the journey lighter and more richer
We will reach the top of this sunny mountain in a few meditated minutes
So please explore and soak up everything you can picture
As you head to its sacred top
. . .
Breath your mountain breaths
Be aware of clouds very much on the same level now
Soothing white peaceful clouds
Ready now
Feel a sense it's time to arrive on the top of the most sacred mountain
Breathing in creamy white sunlight
Connect to this peaceful place and the achievement of getting here
Have a moment more of simply attuning to this height
It's time now for that special meeting to happen
To be fully present with the real you your strength and power of joy
Your inner child

Whom you may find sitting in a meditated state
Take the weight off your feet and rest here
Feel yourself seating opposite each other
For your inner child wishes to be sincerely in total eye lock with you
Let their eyes look deeply into yours
For this is your inner child telling you
How much they love you love you love you
Through this journey and the journey of life
Getting closer to your inner child
Time to eat those golden apples too together
Let the cheeks of the mouth fill with sweetness
As you feel more and more connected and whole again
And strengthening together with the power of love and power of joy
Your own self support
Drink up the golden sunshine on this mountain top.
Look and stare how glorious the sky colours are fantastic clouds
And you are invited to meditate on this grand mountain together
To awaken the extraordinary uplifting qualities of your gifts
So please enter your private mountain together now
You have 1 minutes to re-bond
. . .
Feeling really special now
Now let the balance of work and play begin

Having now the beautiful bond with your inner strength and power of joy
really know yourself
The importance of play time and the rewards of work through life
And with thanks to this mountain for being here for you both
And allowing this special time together
Feel recharged and ready to move on together now
Then with thoughts of your playful inner wishes for a return journey home
But for it to be easy down this mountain with a playful slide
So let there be
Be a smooth winding flowing slide going around and around
Down this mountain to take you back to the ground to that old apple tree
Allow to feel happy & playful with wind in your face sliding down
For the next 30 seconds
. . .
Rolling onto to the ground with laughter inside and feeling whole again
It's time to stand once more under the old apple tree
And pick a golden apple
Eat this fruit and feel it's sweetness in the cheeks of the mouth
And swallow it's nectar & thanks to the apple tree

Feel complete that you yourself have the wonderful uplifting qualities of you
To balance the work with play beautifully
May you continue your journey of life strong and happy
Connect once more to your breathe
Feel it flow in and out
Let's awaken to the count of seven
1234567
Waking up now
Refreshed happy
Eyes opening
Eyes fully open and bright
Thank you

DRAW WHAT YOU SAW

IN **I CONNECT TO MY INNER JOY AND STRENGTH**

A JOURNEY BACK TO WELLNESS PART 1

Welcome to **a journey back to wellness part 1**

Please get relaxed lay down fully get comfy and close your eyes
Now connect to your breath and simply follow the next 3 breaths
. . .
Support often is the key to bring hope back to you
We have to acknowledge when we are not fully well
Often it is a sign for help getting ones strength back and in a sense healing of yourself
Your energies your mind and body gaining balance and belonging
The following is good in stages hence repeat them
To reinforce a surge of positivity that you rightfully deserve
So we will work with your energy system regardless of what the situation
For we are born with a life force system all of us
We all have energy chakras we all have an aura and we all have roots
Let's get to work on your entire energy system and simply make it shine
By focusing on the problem we thus focus now on the answer
See me as your support and we will begin this first part of the journey
And it is a journey for we shall leave the home shortly to visit the lady of miracles
With the eyes closed now thank you

We can expand the mind energy and take that journey within
So think about the home you are in and the front door for leaving the home
Remember how that front door looks and as your support we stand now there together
Ready to go out
There will be a new path outside to follow
Now I'm taking a small picnic hamper for we will rest half way
Before we meet the lady of miracles
She knows we are coming
And the time we get there will always be the right time
So stepping outside the home we begin this walk this journey on this sacred path
That stretches into the distance with tall green grass edges at each side
The walk itself is peaceful the air smells earthy and flowery
For nature is always outside the sun is warming as time passes by a mile down this path
And yet another mile passes by and so we refresh ourselves with a sweet picnic
Of tasty snacks and long cool drinks
Then decide a small gift of wild flowers would be nice to present to the lady of miracles
Just a few will do of delicate beautiful wild flowers
So as we begin again to walk the sacred path
We head upwards towards a hill with a wooden hut that has smoke coming out its chimney

There are 2 horses here grazing near the front wooden door
So the 2 apples left in the basket we decide to share them
And enjoy a moment of these incredible huge but gentle horses that feel wonderful to stroke
Then it's time to knock on the door so I sit back and watch you
Knock 3 times and flowers ready too
The lady that opens the door immediately reveals her name to you
And introduces herself as Betty
Her name is old like the wisdom in her and she smiles very brightly
And as the most beautiful green eyes that are wide open sparkling at all of you
And with a thank you she takes the flowers
and smells and breathes them in
And places them in her window and takes your hand and sits you around the open fire
Then closes her eyes holding your hand
For she is understanding you and your reason for here
And she says although you have been hurt and hurting you like all who come here
Must understand the bad emotions the hurtful emotions are energy stealers of your life force
And your right to shine to feel the magic of yourself
So we will let it all go and let it drift into the past for your future holds great happiness
Wonderful things the miracles of life

We will begin to purge then ground you today
A white feather lands on your lap that is actually a pen
A sheet of paper drifts onto the lap too
And the fire crackles ready to burn the words of emotions
The words that have caused these things to you
So she will count to 3 to signal you to write brief words of troubles
So that everything in black and white is listed quickly
She mumbles time heals all and emotions die only logic remains
Lessons and wisdom will reign
She counts down to 3 for you to begin to write for next 30 seconds
1 2 3 and write
. . .
For the flames grow hungry in the fire ready to burn it all
And leap out and take the paper out of your hands and gobble them up
A gust of black smoke goes up and up the chimney
And your hands are simply empty now
She smiles and gives you a tonic to drink to replenish your energies
She assures you you will feel better after drinking it for peace and love is your reward
It's time to ground you she says
And you and I and the 2 horses that await us outside will take us to the centre of this forest

The ride on the horses is comforting
But the journey is rugged for nature is very deep here
But the centre of the forests has a beam of constant sunlight almost a circle
That lights the ground and at its very edges are wild grasses in a perfect circle
She tells you to stand in it you must ground yourself completely
And claim your place on Earth
With these words the feet themselves born 10 new shoots of roots from all the toes
And begin to bury themselves into the earth
And grow long and keep on growing and growing pulling and growing
And pulling the whole body solid and balanced to the forest floor the roots feel alive
And seek the centre of Mother Earth to anchor you
She encourages you to smile and start to feel incredibly strong and balanced
And just as you hit the centre of Mother Earth the roots tie and anchor themselves there
She test your body by lightly touching you and sees you are rock solid
She reminds you life is long
Miracles happen every day some are very small
Yet are miracles
Some are big miracles big moments in life
And this is one of them this is your full grounding today

Wild grass leans towards you bowing and waiting for you to speak
Then you remember you have much to do with this life
And your roots are free to walk the earth
So an energy of abundance whirls up your roots
The abundance of energy whirls getting stronger but light and come out of the ground
And light up your entire aura
The aura in a sense is the shape of the world for a full round energy completes you
And you are fully aware of your entire body you feel a strength and a surge of happiness
Laughter from the heart radiating in all of you in the roots the body the aura the eyes sparkle
And you breathe in this forest with love and gratitude
She ushers you to come back to the horses and head back to her home for all is in divine order As you get on the horse you feel all the Joy of this beautiful animals
You see all the beauty of the road back in the scenery around you
And then feeling the warmth of the hut and the smell of the open fire sitting back in the chair
She tells you to close your eyes and wish yourself back to your home
For it will save time and she will be here when you are ready to complete the next journey

So your support friend sits beside you as you think of home
Home sweet home and we are both back at the front door of your home
And see yourself laying and resting in your home
You have rested fully whilst your mind expanded
And are ready to refresh yourself with a glass of water

DRAW WHAT YOU SAW

IN **A JOURNEY BACK TO WELLNESS PART 1**

A JOURNEY BACK TO WELLNESS PART 2

Welcome to **a journey back to wellness part 2**

We shall again leave the home shortly to visit the lady of miracles
So please lay down get totally relaxed and close your eyes
And breathe deep and long and just notice the next 2 breaths breathing in and follow
With the eyes closed we can expand the mind energy and take that journey within
So think about the home and the front door for leaving the home
Remember how that front door looks and as your support
We stand now there together ready to go out
There will be that sacred path outside to follow now I'm taking a small picnic hamper
For we will rest half way before we meet the lady of miracles she knows we are coming
And the time we get there will always be the right time
So stepping outside the home
We begin to walk on this sacred path that stretches into the distance
With long grass edges at each side the walk itself is peaceful
The air smells earthy and flowery for nature is always outside
The sun is warming as time passes by a mile down this path and yet another mile passes by
And so we refresh ourselves with a sweet picnic of tasty snacks and long cool drinks

Then decide a small gift of wild flowers would be nice those lovely delicate beautiful flower
To present to the lady of miracles so as we begin again to walk the sacred path heads upwards
Towards a hill with a wooden hut that has smoke coming out its chimney
There are 2 horses here grazing near the front door
So the 2 apples left in my basket we decide to share them
And enjoy a moment of these incredible huge but gentle horses that feel wonderful to stroke
Then it's time to knock on the wooden door so I sit back
And watch you knock 3 times and flowers ready too again
Betty the lady of miracles opens the door thanks you for the flowers
But carries them with you holding your hand to another room
So walking past the fire room that was in journey part 1
You both enter a great unimaginable large hall with a ceiling so high
You can't see quite where it ends
She tells you this is the colour hall room of the 7 human rainbow chakras
We're going to have some fun and colour in all your chakras and they are ready for you
And in a way a new chapter in your life
We need to fill in first your red base energy system

Red represents life the high ceiling here's this and takes on a magnificent vibrant red colour
And starts to fill the room with pure brilliant red
It automatically finds your base chakra
Filling spinning cleansing and most of all
Nourish it with life force energy of red
So keep welcoming it in she says feel the red taste the red breathe in
Red for it is life itself now she checks you by telling you to breathe out a long breath
And a fantastic red air streams out of your mouth
Good now the high ceiling transform once more to sparkling orange
Bright energy orange colour starts to fill the room
Breath it in for it too will automatically find your sacral chakra
Filling and spinning and cleaning and nourish it welcome it in feel d orange taste orange for it is represents order........
Now she checks you by telling you to breathe a long breath out
And a glorious orange air streams out of your mouth very good
Then the high ceiling transforms to the new colour of golden yellow
This yellow bright energy fills up the room and automatically finds your solar chakra
Filling spinning cleansing and nourishing it
So welcome it in tasting yellow feel yellow breath yellow for it represents wisdom
She checks you by saying breathe a long breath out

And a bright full yellow air streams out of your mouth good she says
So once more the high ceiling turns a glowing fresh green colour that fills the room
And automatically enters your heart chakra filling spinning cleansing it and nourish it
So welcome it in breath green taste this green feel the green for it represents love
She checks you by saying breathe out a long breath
And a full green air streams out your mouth good
Now the high ceiling turns to a bright turquoise colour filling the entire room in tortoise air
Breathe it in for it will automatically finds your throat chakra
And filling spinning cleansing and nourish it so welcome it in
Feel the turquoise taste it for turquoise represents power
She checks as you breath out a long stream of turquoise air good nearly there now
And so the high ceiling again turns the colour indigo blue and fills the entire room
In beautiful indigo blue
So breath it in for it will automatically find your third eye chakra
And filling spinning cleansing and nourish it so welcome it in for it represents imagination
She checks by saying breathe out long and a long stream of indigo blue air comes out
Good now for the last colour

And the high ceiling turns now, a purple colour a gorgeous deep purple fills the room
For it will now automatically find your crown chakra
Filling spinning cleansing nourish it feel the purple taste the purple
So welcome it in for it represents oneness with all creation and you're self
She checks by saying breathe a long breath out
And the colour purple air streams out of your mouth
The great hall returns to a natural air and she summaries the end of the task
By asking you to breath now all the 7 chakra colours one by one so she can see
So you start to breath out the base colour red and connect to life
Then the next breath out is orange connecting to order
Then the next breath out yellow connecting to wisdom
Then another breath out green connecting to love
And the next breath out turquoise connecting to power
and the next breath out indigo blue connecting to imagination
And finally breath out purple connecting to oneness with all and oneself
She is pleased for you for you will have so much fun

And so much energy in your life now that all chakras are full and flowing
And now
Simply close your eyes and think of home sweet home
And think of the door front door standing with your support
And we stand there
And then you see yourself laying down
And you know it's time to once more awaken
And drink some water
So at the count of 4 reawakening
1234 eyes open

DRAW WHAT YOU SAW

IN **A JOURNEY BACK TO WELLNESS PART 3**

EARTH SLEEP

Welcome to this guided sleep meditation
Called **Earth Sleep**
Let's begin
Begin a wonderful sleep and dream
It's good to refresh your pillow
So please Squeeze that pillow for sleep and dreams to begin
settle into bed
Stare if you wish a few seconds like everything today has stopped now
..
Closing your eyes thank you
Let empty the mind 10 seconds now
..
Take a long breath in
And that long breath out
Your physical body can begin to recharge
So let's tense the feet a few seconds now
Then tense the long legs a few seconds
Tense the abdomen a few seconds
Please tense the arms hands and shoulders a few seconds thank you
Now really have a long tense of your face hold that face tight anyway you wish
Getting ready to let go
So let go now
Comfy comfy
Follow me to a place that gives so much peace natural beauty and in a way
is medicine to mind and body for all you go through

Recharge as I take you to the forest to sit there
Let there be on one else here
It is trees plant life the nature of birds the gentle things
Find a spot to sit
and notice new plants growing that are still young soft and fresh almost glowing bright green
It really is time to watch a snail go up a tree
Catch that breeze with a butterfly upon it
No one to talk to or to listen to
Just the earth this forest alive
and continues to grow
It's time to notice tallness of trees around you
You may touch one just by reaching out
Most trees feel warm to the touch
When we embrace a tree it is silent, yet it visually speaks to us
Sometimes we can even tell them are deepest secrets
And feel a release in doing so
So I invite for you for 30 seconds only
To let anything you wish to say to be released upon it now thank you
……
And now let's let go of everything and put your roots into this forest
As you sit there
Little roots begin to flow into the ground
As little fresh new leaves open onto the body
It is a moment of great stillness
As you stay here and become the tree you are

Your roots will beneath the surface introduce their selves to the forest
Of hundreds of mighty ancient trees of wisdom
They are thousands of years old
And will bow to great winds and survive
and thrive in new heights
Please join these trees as you deepen your roots
but also grow directly upwards
Sky high
All your new leaves grow on to your branches
Your silence is nothing more than inner peace and life's wisdom
Feel that first breeze
That first sway for you are flexible
Let your heart be captured by the tiniest of birds
That land on your arm your branch
The delicate lightness of such a tiny bird rests on your tree
But something exciting is also coming
For special wild big cat loves to sleep in the forest of trees
And simply picks yours
You are looking absolutely irresistible
And notices a good strong high branch to climb up to
Mother Earth always provides a home for its animals
So welcome this big smooth and soft big cat
To rest here with you
Remember this tree your tree is strong
Well-grounded and so high

So as the big cat does rest and closing those eyes
You can listen to the heart beating now so gentle
Strong yet gentle
As you both wait for a new day to arrive
May the stars shine onto your both
Silver moon shine dips all around your leaves
And sleep and dreams high as the night sky
Dream your very best
Forest sleep And earth sleep Dream of a new day fully recharged

DRAW WHAT YOU SAW
IN **EARTH SLEEP**

TIGER FLYING AND PLANET HOPPING

Welcome to this guided meditation
Called **Tiger Flying And Planet Hopping**
Let's begin
Seated or lay down fully for this one
Closing one eye begin to connect
To the inner and outer you
Closing the eye to begin a fantastic mind journey
Hold the breath still please 7 seconds now
..
Feel that breath long and smooth
The life force energy of you
Please focus and simply wish to be tiny
So tiny
The size of the smallest insect
Let the tiger walk in this room
Who's simply walking through and out
Jump onto the tiger
For you are tiny
Begin a journey
Feels his heart beat
As you snuggle into his tiger coat
Breathe in this fantastic tiger
The tiger is special for he can fly with his mystical wings
And so up and up and up you both fly
Almost like a rocket
Directly upwards
Time to find a new place to be
And that is arriving on a new planet that radiates love

Feel surrounded by energy bubbles of love
The tiger becomes small and continues to shrink
And you begin rapidly to grow back into human form
This new planet is a safe place to be right now
It is love and higher education of wisdom
You are offered something to eat that also quenches you
It's shape and colour is something you've never seen before
But it is powerful in aiding you and gifting you for your future
This being your very own DNA
It's going to fix it and protect it
From earth's annoying virus
The bubbles of energy rush you to digest it
So they can move you onto the next planet
So as you shrink once more to tiny
The tiger grows big again
On you hop and connect and feel his heart beat
As he flies off this planet
Heading a little closer to earth
To land of the realm of the angels of light planet
That looks over earth
This will be deeply therapeutic for you
As you are welcomed by thousands of angels of light
You start to grow again getting bigger
The tiger again shrinks smaller
The angels begin to massage your energies
And unravel any bumps and blockages

As you relax and receive this angelic treatment
Another angel polishes your eyes
Rids anything that is dull
And it feels your eyes that are becoming 2 planets of earth
This is good
For so much beauty and information is in them
The mind is getting a structured energy with survival and manifesting tool added
That will help you to live without fear
But live more productive
The aura requires at least 50 angels to tidy it up
Which for yourself is deeply comforting
Now there's a lot of sparkles happening
For another planet known as the stars is to be travelled to next
So begin to to become tiny once more
And the flying tiger grows big
As you jump on top
Listen and connect to his heart beat
Off to starlight to the star planet
Here is the energy of aiding sleep
And living life as sweet as can be
As you begin to grow and grow big again
The tiger shrinks
Stars begin to connect to your outside
Blasting you with huge bright starlight
The starlight lights up your inside
And every cell in your body is being lit up
As it places the memory the power of sleep and star skies

So your future will involve your bedtime
All you have to do is think
Stars
And the sleep journey will be a galaxy delight
Now the tiger is beginning to grow once more
As you become tiny again
Jump on his back connecting to his heart beat
And flies back to planet earth
He take you to his natural habitat first
The jungle
To nourish and ground you with green plant life
Let your eyes pop out on the huge greenery
Feast your eyes on the jungle green that is growing and growing
And take a swim together in a cool clear stream
And climb a tree and rest a moment upon this tree
You have 30 seconds thank you
. . .
Now the tiger flies once more and takes you back to that room you was first in
And now the tiger simply walks through this room
As you begin to grow bigger and bigger again
Connect to your body feel the hands the feet the body
Tense for a few seconds all your muscles
And relax and hold the breath please 7 seconds now
Now feel that breath long and smooth
Your life force energy
As you open your eyes
Eyes fully open And extremely positive fantastic

And alive thank you

DRAW WHAT YOU SAW

IN **TIGER FLYING AN DPLANET HOPPING**

5 MINUTES TICKITY TOK

Welcome to this short, guided meditation
Called **5 Minutes Tickity Tok**
Let's begin seated or lay down if you wish
5 minutes tickity tock
Though 5 minutes can seem a lot
Every second seems to linger in the air
All meditation is a welcome tonic for the mind
Mind-power doing a million to a zillion things in a lifetime
Go on a journey with me
So soften those blue brown green grey eyes
Let those eyes bow down looking down and connecting to you
Think of the battles you've all gone through
Trials and tribulations karma lessons learnt
Right smack into that beating heart
And that book inside of you waiting to be read
Perhaps you were dormant for a while
The seed that was planted on earth is you and I
Do you remember how bran new you were
The feet barely touched the ground
You ran you skipped you danced you sung
Because life on earth had just begun
The stars shine down to earth for all to see
The quiet time for the night sky keeps us company
For we are never truly alone are we?
Are we not light beings whose mortal body will only shed its skin
For you and I shall travel forever within
Take in a mighty breath

And mighty breath out as if you looped it round the world once or twice
The world has changed as it not?
We're so connected so global
In this lifetime seeing vast changes
For I do not remember as a child having so much
Now what have you seen so far in life it's not just about survival
Have you parachuted?
Sky high from a parachuting plane
Gone horseback riding on a huge white horse on that long sandy beach
Drank champagne
Have you been in hear shot of the roar of a lion that echoes the distance of a mile
Have you held a bird of prey at arm's length and felt it's delicate weight
Have you been to a concert singing together with over a thousand voices
Have you saved a life, or did someone saved yours?
Have you met someone who's reached one hundred years old?
Have you fallen in love, and did you have to fall in love again?
The human life's journey with a mystery end
The world is big and so is the mind big
Life is breath
Take a breath with me of rainbow light
The rainbow colours for they do exist
Take another breath in the colour red and orange
And exhale red and orange let it linger in the air

Take a breath in the colour yellow and green
Exhale that yellow and green let it stay there
A breath of turquoise and exhale turquoise out into the air
Breathe in the colour blue and the colour purple
And exhale that blue and purple to linger and linger
Lastly my favourite a breath in of white light
Exhale white light into the air
Let's finish with one united breath in of pure white light
And exhale pure white light let it enlighten
And wrap you in its tender loving care
This room is full of love and light
Your soul is full of love and light
And those beautiful eyes to the soul
It's time to lift open
Those blue, brown, green greys eyes
At the count of 3
123

DRAW WHAT YOU SAW
IN **5 MINUTES TICKITY TOCK**

HELP ME SLEEP MY BLUE ANGEL

Welcome to this sleeping guided meditation
Called **Help Me Sleep My Blue Angel**
Let's begin
Let's begin this great support
This angel support that is here for you now
And always
Please be ready tucked into bed
Let's change bedtime into your sanctuary
Get comfortable with your pillow your bed
Please close the right eye now thank you
Then the left eye closing it too thank you
Have a dreamy roll round and round clockwise
. . .
And then all the way round anti clockwise
. . .
Relax now resting let's get ready
For this great uplifting Blue Angel to support you
Focus
Focus with heart and mind
A Blue Angel that's all about offering healing
A place of sanctuary through the magic of sleep
And to make that angelic bond
Please For sheer fun give
Give this Blue Angel a personal name
The first name that pops in your mind
That you simply love
. . .
Allow a gentle smile upon your face
Open your heart to the invitation
Of your personal Blue Angel to be present with you to aid sleep time

Hold your chosen name dearly from your heart
Call with your mind this Blue Angel's name 3 times now...

. . .

And in the name of love and light
To help with sleeping secure and positivity well
Begin straight away communicating
With anything you want to release from yourself that is heavy on your mind or heart
Through this Blue Angel listening to you for a minute now please ....

. . .

Now straight away once more communicate
What you wish to improve
Keep it simple but clear for you can always ask another time too
Please proceed now for a minute thank you....

And now to focus on that wonderful angelic support to restful sleep
Simply breathe in now deeply deeply the presence of your Blue Angel
Let blue air fill you up
This angel represents the uplifting qualities and energy of sheer blue
That connects to protection and repairing healing your sanctuary

Then swallow this blue angelic colour over the tongue down the throat
Let it flow sheer blueness
And all the way down through all of you
. . .
Surrender to this wonderful blue glow in the body and and the mind
Breathe in my blue body my blue mind
Expanding now into the pillow
My blue pillow
into the bed
My blue bed
Your Blue Angel
And sealing in a blue angelic bed
Feeling secure lightness blueness
That creates a floaty bluey feeling
Floating is good
Floating in Blue Angel energy
Recharge here
And float for angels are so very light
Just like a great sleep and dreams are so very light
Float into blue sleep
Where the body is so soft
And the dream imagination flows and floats
It is the gateway to the highest of dreams
Your sanctuary
Teaches one the magic of sleep
Sleeping in my Blue Angels light
With love and light
My Blue Angel
Sends me safely to sleep

My Blue Angel watches over me
As I sleep into my highest of dreams
Blue, blue angel
I thank you
(the end)

DRAW WHAT YOU SAW

IN **HELP ME SLEEP MY BLUE ANGEL**

THE TWIN BOYS

Welcome to this guided sleep meditation
Called **The Twin Boys**
Let's begin straight in bed
Lift your arms and squeeze your pillow
This pillow must be very=y comfortable because it's just for you
Get comfy really comfortable
Closing your eyes thank you
Once upon a time 2 young boys grew up very much together simply because they are twins But unidentifiable twins for one was so very thin called John-and his twin brother was twice his size called Peter they hated each other for being different
Mum and dad never really noticed for they behaved so well when in front of their parents
Only behind closed doors did trouble begin
And at school they did a real good job avoiding each other
Or just pretend to be ok with each other
But things were to change
And change for the better
But first something big had to happen
Which happened on a weekend camping family trip
Camping was always fun though
The big outdoors putting up a tent sleeping under stars tucked down in sleeping bags
And going on big, long nature walks
Basically cracking fun plus night time huddled round a lovely fire

Well this time the weekend camping got really scary
As always when exploring both parents took the lead
Whilst the twins walked behind just like a row of ducks
When suddenly far from the camp site and far from anyone else 2 big cries filled the air
As mother and father fell through a good ten feet on the very path they were on
Landing with a bang and thud onto a shallow stony cliff edge
Both boys began to scream but then realised they hadn't really been hurt
They had in fact remained still on the walking path frozen to the spot
Within seconds both parents started shouting but not at the twins but at each other
By blaming one another for being so careless
The twin boys for once almost looked the same as their eyes glazed over in shock
For here was mummy and daddy arguing
A good 5 minutes later they both looked up to the twin boys
For they were sure they could think of a way to get them out of the drop
But how?
Can't climb up too smooth the wall
Can't lift you dear for what will spring you to the top
Nor did they have any rope

Oh dear time to put their thinking caps on
Then Paul said to Peter let's put all our belts together and make a pulling rope
With that mum and dad threw high up both their belts
Then Paul and Pete took their belts and began to lock tight in to each end all 4
Now they was ready for both twins to hold the long belt and dangle it down the side
And mother was first to be pulled by both her boys
It was working then mum and the boys dangled the belt once more over the side
And dad did manage to be lifted up to safety too
By now all 4 had had enough and began to back track back to the camping site
For a special camp fire with lots of songs and a few stories before bedtime
That night both twins suddenly didn't care about being different
But accepted each other once and for all and slept well
After a quick giggle and chat about their parents screaming at each other
Good night sleep tight Paul
Good night twin brother Pete see you in the morning
And goodnight to you sweet dreams too

DRAW WHAT YOU SAW
IN **TWIN BOYS**

PINK BUBBLE OF COMFORT

Welcome to this guided meditation called
The Pink Bubble Of Comfort
Let's begin
Please be seated or lay down if you wish
Let's close those eyes
And just let them free flow moving the eyes inside
Up and down and side to side for half a minute
now thank you
. . .
Let the eyes settle thinking of creating a great pink bubble of comfort
To sooth you and lift you
And holding the breath still now for 7 seconds thank you
Thinking all about pink
. . .
Feel that pink breath long and smooth
Breathing and connecting into pinkness of comfort
Also the natural you that pink is already present
Such as pink finger nails a touch of pink on our daily hands
Toes all lined up in pink
The smile of your teeth sit in pink gums
Even the tongue is naturally pink
And naked lips are blushing pink
Bring a soft smile to the face that loves comfort
The emotion of blushing that signals and rises to pinkness
Little bits of natural pink already truly belong to us
Let's Imagine for a second physically going to a party dressed all in pink

How would you look but how would you feel too?
Feel the pink on the skin
And a smile of just feeling the glow of feeling really good
Breathing the power of pink comfort
But it would be lovely to vibrate high energy pink
So be aware of your true height and shape
For the pink bubble must be the perfect size for you
Let the eyes go foggy with pink colour energy
And then will yourself to glow energy pink
Let's get some extra help with this pink bubble
And invite and welcome in
An Angel of light who is all about comfort
Invite this Pink Angel of your comfort to be present with you
And connect to these words now
in love and light in love and light in love and light
I welcome my angel of comfort
I welcome my angel of comfort
I welcome my angel of comfort
To be with me now
To be with me now
To be with me now
Now welcome this pink angel and
Have a minute letting anything good happen simply accept connect and enjoy
. . .
This angel of comfort loves to help to build a perfect bubble of pink energy just for you
That is all about a hundred percent of comfort

Safe support happy lifting the vibration lifting the mood to fun pink
It's time to own this pink bubble
And be at the centre of it
Bigger than yourself and your aura
It must be a perfect ball shape
Plenty of room for you in it
The qualities of this pink bubble energy supports being in a good mood
Letting life love you back
Let happiness and high comfort be this great pink bubble
All things in a way are bubbles even places situation people
And power belongs to your pink bubble
Deep breath in now of pink energy
Exhale wonderful pink
Feel the love vibration caressing everything in your body your mind and heart
And your life
Accepting everything that feels good and personal to you
Let's float you in that pink bubble with the lightness of your angel of comfort
Filling up with the vibrating pink energy
Connect to sheer lightness
And float in softness
Pink comfort
Let all of you absorb healing pink energy too
Let it dissolve instantly everything that no longer resonates with you

Ask the Angel of Pink energy to lift you even higher in that pink bubble
And shall see you in a couple of minutes enjoy
. . .
And breath into pink
Every nerve ending is swimming in comfort
Every cell of your very being on a quantum level is blushing in pinkness
Breath long and smooth
Blowing pink bubbles
This powerful endless love vibration
Keep holding on to your beautiful, fantastic comfort bubble
Bring it home now
Let's ground this great pink energy into the roots now
Linking now to grounding
And your roots that simply dance all the way happily into the ground
Spreading wide full of comfort and happiness
Sending love into earth too
And she sends her love back
Sending love again to Mother Earth
And she sends back more and more love to you
Feel the aura continues to glow
Glowing fantastic pink
Feel protected supported comforted
Breath into the positivity of pink
And giving thanks to this angel of comfort too
As it is all sealed in
Now for you

We will awake to the count of 8
1 2 3 4 5 6 7 8
Eyes opening
Eyes fully open
And glowing at the centre of your pink bubble
Belonging to comfort
Thank you

DRAW WHAT YOU SAW
IN **PINK BUBBLE OF COMFORT**

MY HEART TONIC ANGEL

Welcome to this guided meditation
Called **my Heart Tonic Angel**
Let's begin
Please get seated or lay down if you wish
And connect to your breath
Hands resting on your heart
Eyes closing and focused
Listen to the heart beat its rhythm the life of this heart
Stay here a minute
Let's
Let's introduce an angel of light right now
Calling your Heart Tonic Angel
To lift your heart
To cleanse it
To feel more connected to it
To motivate and inspire you
I encourage a name to be given to this Heart Tonic Angel
Think of love and allow a lovely name to come to you in next 30 seconds
. . .
And for now moving your hands to open and rested by your side
Welcome in your Heart Tonic Angel to be present
And whilst this happens breathe deeply your colour breaths
Of green and pink
In breathe green
Out breath pink
Have a minute
With in breath a vibrant fresh green like spring grass
And the outbreath like the first pink blossom

Keep it fresh your colour breaths
Focus now on your heart and support from your Heart Tonic Angel
Ready to lift it and cleanse it
And keeping this angel work light and magical
Let all dust and strings and weights be removed Instantly
Removing shadows old stale stuff that is wasting your time
Let your heart tonic angel retrieve it all and really clean your heart up
Help your angel by connecting yourself to wanting to be lighter
Feel grateful for this angelic help
Let your happy angel bring in now a mighty drum
So your heart beats strong
This in a way helps to bounce off your heart anything that isn't from a source of the highest of love
Let your angel bring in the heart power symbol of a lion for standing in your power
Smile as you welcome it in
Let your angel bring also for your higher heart
The power symbol of a unicorn for sheer upliftment
Smile again as you welcome it in
And now to bring in and build a reconnection to everything that has already happened
And worked out for you in your life so far
Breathing into your successful hearts
Let your angel bring in
8 rays of light
To sit in each corner of your hearts
Let your angel bring in 2 healing crystals that hold a rainbow in them

To cushion and support your hearts
And now together these hearts beating the emotion of the highest strongest of love
Let it boost and flood all your body
Filling in all parts of you
A gigantic wave of love as one
Feel the hands and fingers connecting to the highest of love
And continue up the arms with the sensation of great love filling them in
All the chest area the throat the head
Filling with the vibrion of a strong powerful love
Follow this new love vibration filling up the very core of you abdomen
And shooting down the legs stretching wide into all corners of the body
The feet and toes filling with vibrant love
Then feel the heart itself is singing
And your higher heart is dancing
Then a wave
A gigantic wave of love as one
Rolls into the aura
This big wave of love pushing out all stagnation
Pushes out all low vibrations all blockages
And pulsating right now a huge, beautiful love energy
Breathe and feel this love is limitless
Is pure goodness
Is the most exciting thing you have and poses in your life
Focus on the sheer magic and state of being in love with yourself
And in love with life
Then ask your heart angel to seal it in with blessings

Let it enhance your world
Stay lifted
Heart is singing
Higher heart is dancing
It strong it is wise it lights your day every day
Take a breath in and travel with this great heart
Go up with your heart tonic angel and celebrate this new vibration
Stay here for a minute in rejoice of your clean energised sparkling beautiful hearts ......
Bring your breath back to green and pink
In breath fresh green
Out breath blossom pink
Then finally connect to your 2 healing crystal
That are cushioning and supporting your hearts
With 2 rainbows right at their centre
Shining out rainbow light over your entire body
You are the power of love
Love is always the answer to everything
May a new connection to life begin
Be more motivated determined
Appreciating all the little things as much as the big things
Feel you can achieve with your cleansed vibrant hearts
The special personal things that is the unique you

Getting ready to ground to earth now
Think of earth has so special
Send your love to Mother Earth's heart centre
Make a connection make a loving bond
The magic of the sacred number 3

Your heart your higher heart and Mother Earth's heart
All connecting and connected now
Bring your hands to rest once more on your heart area
Connect to that sweetness of your breath
Deep breath in of fresh spring green
And out breath blossom pink
And deep thanks and gratitude to your heart tonic angel
For working with you
Let's awaken to the count of 3
123
Eyes opening up
Eyes fully opening
Keep happy and lifted
Please drink some water soon

DRAW WHAT YOU SAW
IN **MY HEART TONIC ANGEL**

MY YIN YIN MY YANG BACK INTO BALANCE

Welcome to this guided meditation

Called **My Yin My Yang Back Into Balance**

Let's begin

Please get comfortable seated or lay down if you wish

Wrap yourself in comfort and support

Closing the eyes

And connect to the breath with some deep long inhales and long exhales

Go as deep as you can with these power breaths

.....

And relax the breath now into calmness and stillness

Let's begin with connecting to the sun

It's time to connect to the sun the sun energies

For we all have A natural craving of its warmth it's brightness

Its longevity of hours of sun shine days

Heat that lasts all day

To be present now almost a cream yellow light

One of the most exciting lights is being captured in sunshine

Remember how it illuminates all things to be brighter and brighter

Connecting to a perfect sun rise

And all that orchestra of birds singing rising together

Then the perfect sun set a mind blowing super orange fire ball

For the sun really connects to our inner happiness

Bringing an awareness now that sun is a masculine energy

And this masculine energy

That belongs also to the right side of the body

For we are always a balance of yin and yang

How does it feel to give yourself permission

To step your body into that masculine body

Explore this for a minute .....

. . .

The sun is masculine fire

Is light itself your natural yang energies

Connect to your right side of the body now

By tensing all this side of you for ten seconds

Squeeze now into your masculinity .....

Let's focus now on some wonderful qualities that-are here to balance you

Connecting to some precise qualities

For masculinity the protective you

Feel a shift in your energy field

That part of you that is logical

Being strong when needed

That source of direction in life

Connect also to fastness for fast is your masculine yang energies

The structured you

The giving you

The focused you

The stable you

The independent self

The discipline self

The confident you

Your natural awareness

Breath in now sun light as if it touch your lips 7

And you swallowed it in with air

Guide that ball of sun light down the right side

And fill your yang energies

Let half the body your right feel lit up with sunshine......

. . .

Let it connect to the fire energy

And burn away anything that no longer serves you......

Spend a moment here with fire and light and sun

.....

Now Let the right foot plant itself in the ground

Into the hard ground fill yourself up with strength

Like a tree that is old and strong and full of wisdom

Full of life giving energies

Feel the height that a mature tree reaches

It's crown bathed in sunshine

Give thanks to your male energies available to you

Have a moment longer here with all these unique energies..

That support you…….

. . .

Let's connect to the moon now

The moon the feminine energies

This connects to dark

And water energies

The comfort of night bathed in moonlight silver light

And always stars silver stars with that glorious moon

We can look so fully at all her shape

Perfectly silhouetted against that dark blue night sky

Every stage of the moon is so clear to see

We can look up to her and let things go

We can look up to her and bring new things in

Here is the yin energies

Of the female the white perfect white moon

Our fascination magical powers and conquering

Exploring and travelling to the moon itself

Let's focus once more

And connect to the left side of the body now

Giving permission to step into the female energy body

Explore this for a minute...

. . .

The female energies of the left side of you

And squeeze and squeeze all the left side the muscles

Hold for ten seconds connecting

. . .

Relax and melt into the full female into the body

And some wonderful qualities here to balance the yin energies

Precise female energies of water

And of dark

For their must be day and night

The creative you

The nurturing female you

The receiving and sharing energies of yin

The part of you that is all about surrender

The tender you

The sensitive you

The slow and patient you

The empathy

The sensual you

The intuitive self

And the flowing of being female is to flow

Breathe in now moonlight silvery white light

Slow and smooth into the left side of yourself

A white moon shining inside all the left of you

Yin energies are water energy

Flowing through

Let the left foot connect to the softness

Of water

Such a cleansing soothing sensation

Immersed in water

That splash that ripple

Sensual and nurturing

The qualities of cleansing with water

Give thanks to the female energies

That complete you

Spend a moment here longer to your support of yin energies

. . .

Let's connect them both now

And breath into these 2 beautiful energies

Of yin of yang

Of sun of moon

At the count of 3 Breath in feminine 123

At the count of 3

Breathing out masculine 123

At the count of 3 Breath in sun 123

And at the count of 3

Breathing out the moon 123

The balancing of my energies myself

Picture yourself for a minute complete

Whole and complete

The self

That is sun that is moon

Fully recharged now

Flowing better

Nice deep breath now

Fully exhale

Let's awake to the count of 10

1 2 3 4 5 6 7 8 9 10

Waking up now

Eyes opening

Fully open

Wide open

Have a gentle stretch Please drink some water and thank you

DRAW WHAT YOU SAW

IN **MY YIN MY YANG BACK INTO BALANCE**

CHANGING ANXIETY MEDITATION

Welcome to **Changing Anxiety Meditation**
Please get very comfortable in a comfortable chair or lay down if you wish
And wrap yourself in comfort .....
Please take a deep full breath and hold for 4 seconds
Release slowly slowly empty your breath
Closing the eyes
In fact squeeze the eyes shut and relax the face into relaxation
And be very aware of your entire head this thing that navigates one through life
Please breath in change
Exhale change
Breath in changing anxiety
And exhale changing anxiety
Feel that need to change and rearrange the furniture inside your very head
To dust down and chuck away the worn out beliefs of oneself
That's right see the very head needing a positive uplifting change
And rearrange the furniture you call home inside your very head
See dusting down and chucking away old very old beliefs of oneself
Link to playfulness lightness and redecorate your inside
The mind the head with new furnishings just accept the best a comforting self-support
And how to do this with anxiety too

Many things we simply do on auto pilot we simply do this
Certain things inside almost like a computer churn out old programs
That no longer serve you fully anymore
For life is often about change improvements
See and imagine now the neural pathways that anxiety run up and down on
That your subconscious mind put so very much in place
It was once your protection from life's infections
Feel it is time to blast and clear it out with a luminous light rid the shadows
Keep the pathway neural pathway
But rid its old messages empty out the old anxiety causing nothing but bother
And give yourself permission
And fill it with assertiveness and human hope fill it up with goodness
Feel you are changing updating and filing and filling that neural pathway with new assertiveness
A direction full of lightness creativity and change
See those automatic pilot pathways changing for the better
And feed the brain the body let it enjoy a new ride with a splash of fun
Reboot your self-belief system you deserve it and let it be done
Let the head be home to your loving positivity and the best of energies
Breath in good feelings good decisions

Starting a fresh a solid foundation and love your new direction
Opening up to the real you
Full of positivity and the powerful lightness of focused assertiveness
Linking yourself to great things
Wiring up to the being brilliant and happy achieving through believing
Your head will love this new way of thinking staying on a high vibrational flow of assertiveness Positivity connecting to all good things
See the head home with new furnishing that pleases you invites you empowers you
Making life better and better
Focus staying focus
A new automatic positive me the assertive me
My new neural pathway full of a new way of thinking feeling good
Linking opening my talents strong and proud
Tapping into fun expanding the mind the head to work in a positive way through life
Seeing the world as my oyster claiming wonderful things to happen
Feeling solid in my new foundations
Grounded to a very colourful world
That I am a part of
Self-mastery of the wonderful awesome me
And at the count of 3 opening up to real awesome me
1 23 ready to be fully awake eyes open have a great life feeling bright as the star you are

DRAW WHAT YOU SAW
IN **CHANGING ANXIETY MEDITATION**

YOUR VOICE AND YOUR LIGHT BLUE CHAKRA

Welcome to this guided meditation
Called
Your Voice And Your Light Blue Chakra
Let's begin
Seated or lay down if you wish
Let's close the eyes
And Let the eyes inside begin and continue to free flow left right up down
. . .
Let's get to know the true power of all the things your throat and chakra does
That ripples into your life
The life breath our voices all communication and the essence of creativity
Eyes now settled centred
Now Fear
Is the very opposite of creativity creation
But every one of us is this very thing
So letting go of fear walk away from it into the safety of your own powerful divine creation
Time to quickly paint the room you are in now into white
With your imagination the mind
So every wall beautiful empowering white
Paint that ceiling into a white ceiling
And the floor a soft energy carpet of white
Lastly the physical self
Let everything that is touching you and
Supporting the body be clothed in energy white
Comforted in this lovely white space
Recharging here in your white energy space

Know you too are pure energy and stay here half a minute thank you
Let's honour your throat area moving onto colour
Blue is deeply healing a true energy colour for all healing work
With your imagination the mind
Change every wall turning them into lovely light blue
Turning the ceiling fully into sky blue
And a energy light blue carpet floor
Let everything touching you and supporting you connect to light blueness
Soak up this healing energy colour
Let it travel as healing energy
To the precise physical throat areas
Of the mouth....the teeth and gums... the jawline... the vocal cords
The throat the ears the neck and shoulders and muscles ....
And as this healing blue energy continues to happen
Let's open this light blue chakra of the throat
Will it command it
To open
Tell this chakra to spin spin faster
Tell it cleanse itself
And to come back into balance
Creating now some loving energy around this area
Let the face soften and gently rise into oneness
And welcome in to receive this great energy blue and swallow it up

Breathe it out blue air
Please continue for half a minute fully focused on blue breaths in and out now thank you
. . .
The 5th throat chakra connects to the 5th element of ether space
The others elements being earth fire water air
But Ether is both nothing and everything
The very thing that makes all movement and all life possible
And the vast universe is made of ether space
When it is in a balanced state
It induces knowledge and awareness intuition
As light as spirit to understand new and creative ideas
The element ether influences the mind and the heart
When we rest in its silence and emptiness
Have a half a minute of honouring ether and empty your mind thank you
. . .
Come back to the breath
Lots of lovely things empower the throat
Here is
Your Creative identity
Every one of us has a unique creativity
Also speaking ones truth kindly too
When we balance this chakra
We learn to truly listen
A master of clear communication
Living life creatively

The throat is also connected to the essential oils of lavender
And to the taste of bitter foods that act as a cleanser removing natural toxins
Soothing the throat with thyme and liquorice and honey
Cleansing the air and space around us at home with smoky sage
Also connected to certain blue crystals
Such as turquoise blue tourmaline blue lace blue quartz's
Let's enjoy and invite an Angel of light and crystals to energetically
Bring to the throat area and shoulders
These beautiful crystals to sit in your aura to aid its wellbeing
Please connect to these words
Angel of light and crystals
Of light and crystals
Of light and crystals
Be with now in love and light love and light love and light
Have 2 full minute here thank you
. . .

And thank you Angel of light and crystals may these blue crystals continue to stay with you in this meditation
Now working with the throat is to continue life with your communication skills
Things like

Letter writing
Inner child communication
To practice silence
Story telling
Singing
Chanting toning
Release the voice
To physically loosen the neck and shoulders
Keeping a healthy throat chakra through a magical mantra
The singing throat mantra here is H. A. M. H a m
The ham mantra meaning power
Next time sing it standing and to see yourself energetically swaying
Tuning up to the throat chakra
We shall have a little singing but feel free to do this other times too
Let's prepare this with a deep breath and a count up to 3 to sing the mantra ham sound
3 times
Follow me with a deep breath and at the count of 3 to sing ham 3 times
Deep breath
. . .
123
HAM ham ham
Feeling that nourishing vibration
This mantra can be done longer singing it to the sacred number of repeating it 54
Or 108 times to embody the mantra in your energy field

Now learning is a part of life
With the throat learning to overcome obstacles
Such as anger expressed in the throat area
They say when we feel anger in that moment we give our power away
They say the ones we are angry at are drawn into our sphere as mirrors
That reflects parts of us we don't want to see but need healing all healing is empowering
It's about owning and stepping into your power
The opposite of anger is love unconditional love
That is universal
So can we learn to tolerate to be more compassionate to forgive quicker
To avoid also others fragile state too
Learning and controlling anger in the throat is to calm down
And express logically assertively
Physical we can exercise too the tonic of ridding stresses
Problem solving is part of life
That begins really by making peace with our today's
That shall break through to our tomorrow's
This is how we make things happen
Moving up through up vibrational alignment
Letting go of worry topics stop feeding them
So please play the game and start to collect that good list of each day
And watch it grow daily bigger better for all your tomorrow's

Let's focus on a happy throat a happy chakra of light blue
And from time to time to bring your inner child out to play upon it
With sound music singing enriches and powers the throat area
Please explore your favourite music for calming and also for excitement upliftment
Some of your personal favourite music may even go back to the past happy memories
And lastly the power of keeping a journal your personal life diary
The throat the voice your words
Now let's have some fun a tonic let's journey a little
Please connect to yourself as pure energy
Breathe into I am pure energy
And ready to leave awhile the physical body for an uplifting tonic
Think blue and become blue
The biggest blue that we connect with and know really is the sky
That is constantly with us every waking day and each night
Let's reach so very high
So become this pure blue energy and lift up to join the sky and be a part of it
Feel blue feel big and wide
limitless
Stretching flowing as blue skies

Feel you travel and in a way surround this living planet earth
Knowing sky colour itself touches the universe
Breathe in as the ultimate of oneness
Everything is connected
Connect to all good things and go even higher reaching the
Stars
For the throat is very much connected to certain stars
Your 5th chakra links beautifully to the
Star of Venus
Of mercury
Of Uranus and
To Mars
Feel the power of you and your throat light blue chakra
Please have a full minute here
. . .
And breathe blueness
Now let's connect with that sky and
Grab a fluffy white cloud and descend back gracefully to earth
It's time to take this blueprint of upliftment this tonic back home with you
Go back to your physical body
Enter your body once more
With a natural stretch filling into all of you
Feel a rise and stretch into your posture
Declaring I am cleansed I am balanced and empowered

By the human throat it's light blue chakra
My blue throat is creatively happy
Inhale deeply through the mouth over the gums and teeth the jawline the throat shoulders Entering now all your body your life force energy
And now ground yourself
Your roots by thinking feet
That walk the earth
Anchor yourself to earth
Breath in clean and energised
Feel the power of you and blueness
Let's awake to count of 4
1234
Eyes opening
Eyes open
Awake
Why not start making a list of things you like that represent blue
And empower your daily life with blue things
Blessings and
Thank you

DRAW WHAT YOU SAW

IN **YOUR VOICE AND YOUR LIGHT BLUE CHAKRA**

EATING WELL

Welcome to this guided meditation
Called **Eating Well**
Let's begin
Please lay down fully if possible or a seated if you prefer
As you close your eyes
Let the hands
Gently and smooth
Connect to the body and the shape
Listen to everything
As you use the sense of touch
You may wish to stroke your tummy
Feel all the Arms
The legs from hip to feet
We are getting to know the outside that reflects the inside
Breathe into love and light
We all belong to love and light
Ask yourself being a healthy weight is this what you want?
Ask yourself have you ever been a healthy weight too?
Breathe into heart's desire for eating well that is connected to wellness and wellbeing
What is wonderful is our bodies how they naturally change and with sheer will power can change again
Food is foremost a pleasure a necessity too
And brings a much needed break between the work we do
If you truly desire to lose weight naturally and healthy then we come back to the same answer

Exercise and that can be many things combined
with food at sensible portions for energy and
health
But what's happening on the inside on a holistic
approach
We all have within chakras that connect to
everyday life
Let's unblock and lift our chakras to promote eating
well and healthy body once again
First of all is forgiveness that may have affected
you and those around you
Be willing to send this humble word forgiveness to
the inside of you
Staring at the top of the head and forgive whatever
energy is there
Our head chakra connects to the purple chakra
See yourself being freed at last from any low
vibrations
And rewarding yourself with a positive smile
remember change is powerful
Send forgiveness to the next chakra to your third
eye of indigo blue
Free yourself smiling into positivity
Send forgiveness to the next chakra the throat of
light blue colour
Release and free from low vibrations smile again
into wellness
Send forgiveness to the heart chakra colour green
Freedom once more to connect to the instant
action of a smile and its powerful positivity

Send forgiveness to the next chakra the solar chakra of yellow the tummy area
Break away from low vibrations and reconnect to wellbeing
Send forgiveness to your sacral chakra of orange
Move off low vibrations into higher wholesome vibrations of wellness
Send forgiveness to the base chakra of red
Free from stagnation low vibrations back into good, better vibrations you deserve
. . .
Feel a blast of new energy entering around the outside of the body into the aura
The aura is a part of your energies and is receiving an instant relief and pick me up
I want you to imagine smoothing down your aura as if you were combing brushing your hair
Getting rid of blockages and tares and building a new vibrant healthy personal aura
Connect to a smile make it an energy smile that explodes all around you connected to all your life force energy
Train your taste buds to enjoy more natural foods
Treats are here for a reason we earn them and then we enjoy them in a kinder way
Love your tummy be so kind to your tummy so it gets the right portions inside
Then the fun of a little muscle and toning on the outside we can make our tummies strong again for sure

Tell yourself I am in charge of my new world of eating well
And love the me I am becoming
Remember a thousand steps begin with the first step
That all things begin and we will make our dreams come true
Breathe into your energies awakened and happy super positive
And will power I will be well
Now the solar chakra is located in your stomach area and this is also for confidence and self-esteem
As well as helping you feel in control of your life.
This chakra is relates to our personal power and strength
It also governs our pancreas and blood sugar regulation which is important in weight management
The root chakra is about stability, survival, and security just below the hips
It contains the Earth energy
The root is the one most easily stabilized through food so in a way eat your vegetables
That grow in the ground for health and happiness and blessing too
Lets open our eyes to the count if 5
1 2 3 4 5
Eyes opened and focused on you

DRAW WHAT YOU SAW
IN **EATING WELL**

STAR SLEEP

Welcome to this guided sleep meditation
Called **Star Sleep**
Let's begin
Let's begin in your bedroom please

All pillows love a good squeeze to make them big and dreamy
So please squeeze your pillow now good
Please jump into bed now.....
Then Resting your head into the dreamy pillow ....
Closing 1 eye to sleep thank you
Closing the next eye to dream thank you
Squeeze them shut
Good
Let the eyes in side move Up and down Up and down
Then side to side Side to side
Eyes are Ready now to sleep and dream
Let's begin now with your feet and toes
tensing them tight for a mere second
Then tensing your legs tight for a mere second
Then the tummy tensing a little tight for a mere second
Then the arms and hands tensing so very tight for a second
Lastly your head face tensing so tight for a mere second
Now go soft everything into sleepy softness
Yawn if you wish snuggle down
Ready for the magic star sleep to begin
Let's have some fun and prep your bedroom
And paint it soft white with your dream imagination every wall
And ceiling matching in soft whiteness
The bedroom loves to sleep in soft sleepy White
The floor a blank carpet of fluffy whiteness
The pillow too changing to soft whiteness
Everything touching you for sleep time Is turning soft white

Hold the breath still 3 seconds 123
Breathing now my white star bright bedroom
Get really comfy ....
Let's honour the night sky of stars
All the stars are really so physically so very far away up in that big sky
Or maybe not so far away. For they are always always visit you every bedtime
Smiling and sparkling Shining into your eyes
Amongst the starry night sky
One silvery white moon and white floating fluffy clouds on a magical sleeping wind....
Invite into your bedroom the ceiling lighting up with a galaxy of stars
Let your breathing gently connecting to stars and
Star light 1 silvery white moon
And white fluffy clouds floating on a sleeping wind
Let all heaviness disappear and replace with lightness rising in all of you
Softly breathing and connecting to a galaxy of stars
1 white Silvery moon and Fluffy white clouds f
Floating on a sleeping wind breath it all in
And let it travel around the body up and down the body ...
And let it travel around the head side to side In the head..
What a wonderful way to go to sleep
Maybe you can become a star
In the big bedtime sky on your ceiling
Will you be a small star Or the biggest star of them all?
Maybe a family a conciliation of stars

Would you like to fly like a shooting star all night long
Streaming over the silvery white moon
Fast Flying in and out of floating fluffy white clouds
on the sleeping wind
Flying is good floating to sky sleep
Star magic sleep
Will there be any white snow clouds too?
Can you make a snow cloud release lots of white
snowflakes onto the sleeping wind?
So I wish you a magic dream bright sky high
And dream with a galaxy of stars
Keep sparkling all the time
Put a smile on the white silvery moon
And a smile on you
Fluff up those fluffy clouds
Add some snowflakes too time to dream 1 2 3
My magical star sleep
Maybe you can be a star in the sky

DRAW WHAT YOU SAW
IN **STAR SLEEP**

DESTRESS RELAX MY BODY

Welcome to this guided meditation
Called **Destress Relax My Body**
Let's begin
Ready for some deep inner work self-work let's look after you right now
Please get really comfortable laying down if possible or seated fully supported
Wrap yourself in comfort and support that whole body now
Let's Acknowledge the room you are in for just 10 seconds looking around you
And ready to switch off and recharge through deep relaxation
So at the count of 3 close one eye
123
At the count 2 please close the other eye
1 2
Ready for that mind journey to begin
Noticing the rhythm of breath and just stay with that for a moment
. . .
Please take a full deep breath and holding it in for 5 seconds
Smooth and slowly release all that breath
Let's work that wonderful mind and make some changes to do with relaxation
Let's turn this room into an oasis
Simply imagine everything is lifting to a blank canvass of white

Let the energy of pure white be your connection to relaxing now
With the eyes closed we can still roll the eyes up and picture a glowing white ceiling
Breathing in soft white
And roll the eyes down to picture the floor itself mirrors soft relaxing white
Breathing into the glow of white
And the eyes can continue to move under the eyelids side to side and corner to corner Picturing those soft deep relaxing white glowing walls
Breathing into pure relaxing white energy

Imagine as you are laid or seated in a texture of soft whiteness
The pureness the newness of sheer white
Feel the head and the whole body connected to glowing comfort of whiteness
So you are bathed in sunshine white the master colour of relaxing repairing
Healing the mind and body
At the count of 3 please lift one hand up a little
As if pushing it through the air of relaxing white
This master colour of deep relaxation that links beautifully into self-healing
Then relax the hand resting supported comfortable
Focusing now on the face and those expression lines and just decide to soften and relax all of the face letting go into stillness

Soften the eye area dropping all movement into deep relaxation
Bringing a serene relaxed face
Let's invite a gorgeous wave of white light energy to flow through the body
Focus on wave after wave of white energy
Flowing all the way down over and through the body
Start to breathe into these white waves of relaxing energy ....
Breathing down through the body
See the beauty of white waves a healing cleansing energy flowing
Wave after wave down the full length of the body
Now we can link onto the natural laws of the world of gravity
Ready to unload any remaining heaviness
With one big summary of anything heavy from the past or present
That has thought that are heavy or feelings that are heavy you can allow gravity to claim it
Let's let go of heavy thoughts or simply heavy feelings
To start dropping them all to floor level
Let the heavy weight follow gravity to the hard floor
Checking in now and simply start to feel totally lighter and lighter and lighter
This allows the body and mind to feel free once more
Stay here feeling free

Let's acknowledge the body and mind on a quantum level
All the tiny things that makes us whole
Simply meaning billions of cells inside oneself
Let's send one beautiful message to all these billions of cells
Boosted with the master colour white of relaxation repairing and healing
Let's imagine this lovely glow of white air is absorbing
And resonating at master level to those of billions cells
Softly breathing while billions of cells enjoy the light relaxing white air
Maybe you can picture billions of glowing white bubbles
In fact our happiness moments we do truly feel light as air
And the playful sensation of naturally leaping in the air jumping for joy so brilliantly light
Let's thank the body for all it does
Breathing into a billion of lightness
Focusing now on the bone structure
See how wonderful the body is made
See all the bones in perfect position
Feeling smooth and in a sense belong to the colour of white
And how the bones move smooth with every muscle
Welcoming back good posture

And while you relax let the subconscious begins to correct and rebalance the body
Linking into rebalance and let the subconscious all of it now
And dropping any remaining tension inflammation down to the floor to gravity
Let's rest deeply here for a while as the mind rebalances the body itself
. . .
And the gift now of connecting to the power of now right now
Just like the cleanliness of white
The present and future can be supported with lightness and flowing
Keeping bright feel how lightness does smoothly flow all things for mind and body
Let your beautiful mind flow smooth and happily
The balance of emotion and the balance of logic
Let that wonderful body flow with lightness
A mind and body that is truly balanced
We can now move onto to a refreshing start
Setting the intention to feel new again
Positivity is my support

Breath in to positivity and it's creativity and abundance
To flow we also need to drink more water
And look to replenish the body with long drinks of water to flush and cleanse the body soon
Just enough time to set the intention to simply flow that body better when you awake

Focus on your breath now
Breathing in feeling new again and happy
Feeling new and shiny
Breathing into balanced
At the count of 8 waking up to feeling fully recharged
1 2345678
Waking up by connecting to the feet first
By stretching the feet
Feeling attuned to Earth now grounded
Eyes opening
Fully opening eyes now
Wide awake
Let's drink some water soon and good to go
Thank you

DRAW WHAT YOU SAW
IN **DESTRESS RELAX MY BODY**

WELCOME TO YOUR INDIVIDUAL JOURNAL - LET'S DO THIS!

WHAT AGE AND HEIGHT ARE YOU NOW?

WHAT FRUIT AND VEGETABLES ARE YOUR FAVOURITES?

WHAT FLOWERS AND BIRDS ARE IN YOUR GARDEN?

NAME SOME OF YOUR FAVOURITE BOOKS

WHAT MAKES YOU SMILE BEFORE YOU EVEN DO IT?

WHO DO YOU LOOK UP TO?

WHAT DO YOU LIKE ABOUT MUM?

WHAT DO YOU LIKE ABOUT DAD?

HAVE YOU ANY SISTERS OR BROTHERS? PLEASE TELL ME ABOUT THEM!

HAVE YOU ANY PETS? PLEASE TELL ME ABOUT THEM!

WHAT WOULD BE THE PERFECT BIRTHDAY PARTY?

WHAT WOULD BE THE PERFECT HOLIDAY?

WHO ARE YOUR SUPERHEROES?

DO YOU KNOW ANY JOKES?

HOW WOULD YOU DESCRIBE YOURSELF?

PLEASE DRAW A PICTURE OF YOURSELF

DID YOU KNOW SMILES KEEP YOUR HEART MUSCLE HAPPY

AND KEEPS YOU PRODUCTIVE? SO PLEASE DRAW LOTS OF SMILES NOW!

WHAT DO YOU DO AT WEEKENDS?

WHAT IS YOUR FAVOURITE SUBJECT AT SCHOOL?

LOVE AND BLESSINGS TO YOU - DRAW ME A LOVE HEART THANK YOU

About The Author

Born in North Lincolnshire 1966, Linda Owen comes from a large Yorkshire family of seven children. A nature lover by heart, Linda dabbles in poetry. She has entered a personal journey of self-help through holistic therapies and then became a practitioner, a Reiki lady and a natural born storyteller. Her writing has taken on many forms, ranging from different topics of books with the themes of wellbeing, spiritual, poetic and even humorous.

Linda is now working as a meditation teacher on the global website – Insight Timer, with lots of guided meditation stories and although originally for adults, now caters for children too. Her acquired knowledge through time and her age has brought more life wisdom to share.

With her background in holistic therapies, this enabled Linda to get her work (since 2020) out verbally, online and in audio style, benefiting others, covering a wide age group of people who are interested in the holistic approach of natural wellbeing of the mind and body through guided meditations. Then it occurred to Linda that it would be lovely to put all the children's stories together in a book, to enjoy a new experience and become a useful tool to aid sleep time and wellbeing.

Her stories are tender, magical, all about promoting a positive mindset through a positive creative imagination, proving that sleep time may be wholesome, nurturing, and empowering.

https://linda-OWENs-website.yolasite.com/

https://insighttimer.com/lindaowen

book reviews welcomed

Linda Owen

Blessing from Linda Owen x

Printed in Great Britain
by Amazon